Chants of the Higher Soul: A Collection of Elevating Poetry

Kendra Cole

BookLeaf Publishing

India | USA | UK

Presentation by *BookLeaf Publishing*

Web: www.bookleafpub.com

E-mail: info@bookleafpub.com

ISBN: 9789363309999

First edition 2024

ACKNOWLEDGEMENT

To God, the Most High and most worthy to be praised—thank You for Your infinite wisdom and unending grace. Your presence has given me strength in times of weakness, comfort in times of sorrow, and joy in times of triumph. This journey would not have been possible without Your divine guidance and unwavering support. I thank You for Your love and all things.

To Keymn Miles Cole and Kye Maddox Cole—your love and presence are among the greatest motivators for me to strive to become my best self. Your presence and love inspire me daily and your influence is felt on every page of this book.

To my love, Marvin Hemphill, whose unwavering support and wisdom have been a consistent anchor in my life. When I thought I couldn't, you assured me that I could. In moments of doubt, you reminded me that the answers were within me from the start. And when choices need to be made, you say with great faith that Jesus is the way. Your support and wisdom have shaped this journey profoundly, and for speaking life into me - thank you forever.

To everyone who has offered me encouragement and kindness, this book is a reflection of your faith in me. Thank you all.

PREFACE

Growing up as a young Black girl in a predominantly white and affluent community, I quickly understood the feeling of being different. One poignant memory involves a science lesson where the teacher refused to acknowledge anyone speaking out of turn. Desperately needing to use the restroom, I raised my hand but was ignored. Faced with the choice of embarrassing myself or breaking the rules, I chose to walk out, my heart pounding.

I expected reprisal but none came. After using the restroom, I went to the principal's office, seeking solace. The kind principal, a man with a gentle smile and salt-and-pepper curls, listened to my tale and reassured me that I had made the right choice. I had chosen me.

This moment of quiet defiance and self-affirmation is the spirit behind "Chants of the Higher Soul: A Collection of Elevating Poetry." These poems are a testament to the power of choosing oneself and embracing one's worth. May they elevate and inspire you as they have for me.

Walk Tall

Head straight. Walk tall. It's a long and narrow
hall,
As seismic forces yield an earthquake's shake,
Crashing, crumbling fixtures fly off the wall,
Threatening the floor to fall and break.
Head straight. Walk tall. It's a long and narrow
hall.
Trusting yourself or nothing at all.

With fiery haste, akin to answering your calling,
Fueled by love of self, pure and unwavering,
Strobe lights burst from your soul,
Pulsate to the beat of harmonious sounds of
heartsease.
Head straight. Walk tall. It's a long and narrow
hall.
Trusting yourself or nothing at all.

Even when you feel yourself too small,
Trusting your strength and the stillness of calm.
Blessed with the zest of life,
Grateful for each step, enduring all.
Head straight. Walk tall down a narrowing hall.
Trusting yourself or nothing at all.

With Love We Grow

Let it be told,
How life should flow.
There will be roads,
But love will let you know.

Heart be the compass,
Mind steers sure and safe,
Navigating the alleys,
With love who knows the way..

Speak gentle and bold,
Let their eyes behold,
Saturated in life's light,
With the beauty of the soul.

Let it be told,
How things unfold.
Be still and know.
With love, we grow.

If God is in Control

If God is in control, then what are we doing?
Why worry and scheme meticulously
planning, picking, and choosing?
Thoughts become dreams overshadowed by
doubt
Morphed into nightmares
Slowly moving forward unsighted,
Lost in one's irrational fears.
If dreams are the seed, then reality is the fruit.
A firm hand to squeeze extracting from it the
juice.
Given freedoms of choice,
Choose wisely, ambitions set on high
Yield to the Ruler without one's understanding
Leaning into the complexities of purpose,
finding rhythm and reason.
Breathe in the serenity and rest in the now.
Embrace the season.
In quiet, discover ease; let your heart sway.
Trust the process. Merrily find the way.

Quietly Praying

Watching. Waiting
Watching. Waiting.
Quietly praying.
Quietly praying.

Don't start fading.
Don't start fading.

Radiant shine.
A beautiful mind.
Leave it behind
And the heart will go blind.

Watching. Waiting
Watching. Waiting.
Quietly praying.
Quietly praying.

Don't start waning
Don't start waning

Appear as a flower
Though only a seed.
Stretched arms to the sun
Gaining all that is a need.

Watching. Waiting
Watching. Waiting.
Quietly praying.
Quietly praying.

Renovating.
Recreating.

Profess your peace.
Proclaim of your love.
Soul drenched in joy
And the Divine above.

Watching. Waiting
Watching. Waiting.
Quietly praying.
Quietly praying.

Don't start fading.
Don't start fading.

Just Be

If you just be, then you will be
Simply be, and somehow you'll see.
That whatever happens is happening for thee,
If you be you and let me be me.

If you just be, then you will be
Growing abundantly and gracefully,
Bold in self, with inhibitions set free.
You be you. Let me be me.

If you just be, then you will be
Elevating mentally,
Finding peace so exuberantly,
Living life fully, harmoniously.

Celebrate the Day

Early awaken in the day
Get out of your own way.
Eyes on Divine as you pray
Another beginning to celebrate. Celebrate!
Today's the day.
Celebrate.

From your heart let joy escape.
Broadcast the good news all through the day.
Shine up your good shoes and lead the way.
Finding time to celebrate. Celebrate!
Today's the day.
Celebrate.

Come alive in the daylight.
Cast off shadows and embrace the bright.
In togetherness, find your way.
Make each hour a time to play. Celebrate!
Today's the day.
Celebrate.

Affirming Me: I Am Affirmations that Empower

I am created because I am the best.
I am the victor, and blessings manifest.

I am here with the purpose, to impart
Blessings to the lives that I touch and spark.

I am deserving. I am cherished.
With divine support, my limits perish.

I am kind. Divine goodness in me grows.
I reflect His glory in all that shows.

I am a giver, ready to receive
Everything that destiny has conceived.

Live On (A Chant of Perseverance)

Magnify the joyous echoes as the highest
mountains sing:
Well done, my friend, well done.

The warmth of the sun and gentle winds that
bring,
Keep on, my friend, keep on.

In the trees, an abundance of its fruit unfolds.
Well done, my friend, well done.

Fill your cup with peace and truth like gold.
Live on, my friend, live on.

Arise!

Dreamer,
A world awaits its dawn within you —
So you must arise.
The richest of kingdoms lives in you.
Open up your sleeping eyes,
Awaken your mind —
Arise!
The world needs you now. Arise!
Wake up, wake up, somehow. Arise!

Dreamer,
Your path is set with tasks to be done —
So you must arise.
Only you can see the battles won.
Step forward with valiant pride,
Awaken your mind —
Arise!
The world reaches out. Arise!
Find your strength, somehow. Arise!

Dreamer,
For you, in this world, there is a place.
So you must arise.
No running, no hiding, no sleep to take,
Claim your stake, take your prize —

Awaken your mind —
Arise!
The world needs you now. Arise!
Wake up, wake up, wake up — Arise!

Be Free, Run Wild

Let's take a while, letting our hearts,
Be free, run wild...

Feel the wind's whisper, the moon's soft glow,
Under starry skies, where wild things grow.

I need you,
By my side, for the ride.
Be my guide, running wild.

I need you, I need you,
I need you, I need you...

Stay with me now, light a fire,
In the cool night air, where our desires transpire.
Free your mind, running wild.

I need you,
By my side, for a time.
Untamed; running wild.

I need you, I need you,
I need you, I need you...

Stay with me, with hearts combined,

In this fleeting time.
Let's run through fields, feel freedom's breath,
Together in joy, escaping the rest.

Let's take a while, letting our hearts,
Be free, run wild...

Love is the Dopest Thing

Love is luxurious,
Prime location real estate,

Taking the best of me
Revealing all mistakes.

Carry you from point A to B,
No guardrails in the way.

Love is the most ambrosial flavor
That you will ever taste.

Love is the grandest place
That you will ever stay.

Love is the loudest song
You will ever play.

Love is the dopest thing,
Forever and a day.

Where You Belong

The road is outstretched and winding,
Dangerously rising
Asphalt sharply turning
Blindly as it goes.

Drifting forward swiftly
Climbing ever so gently
Engine heavy lifting
Stronger as you go.

Anticipating detour
Traveling through turmoil
Through alleyways,
Arriving at the time and space
Precisely where you belong.

A Plea to Lead

Evicted from Eden he led her
Knowing now which way to go
Clueless of Earth's cruel expanse,
Escaping God's garden's last glance.

Retreating to a cave is all they know,
Trembling from the serpent's sinister blow.
'Now we must go.' said he in sorrow slow.
'Where, I do not know.' To her, his weakness
shows.

'We are strayed and led astray.'
'And I am afraid'
'Dismayed and frail today,'
'Too weak to lead the way.'

As they embraced, a tearful start,
Fear in her eyes, truth in her heart.
She met his gaze with grief and plea,
Trust Him. Abandon your fear. Rise to your
calling. Lead me.

Release + Reclaim

Let's go! Let go!
Release the tempest from your soul.
Let anger fade,
Let go of doubt.
Bring peace from within,
Breathe the worries out.
Dismiss every fear,
Blame cast out.
For heartbreak will heal.
Shedding the scales of shame.
Release and reclaim.
Unburden yourself
Let it rain.
Let it be.
You are well,
You are free.

Awaken to Joy

Awaken joy in the simple things.
Awaken love and all that it brings.
For you may never know
The next time you may sing.
Awaken, soul, to my highest plane.

Crown of Resilience

Move as if nothing weighs you down,
With faith so strong, you bend but not break.
Carry on without worry or frown,
For all weapons against you will drown,
As long as you wear your crown.
Immunity to all that compromises your truth,
You are the proof:
That diamonds need pressure
That rain gets no wetter,
That things will get better—
Better than ever.
Reap all the good within you,
For wherever your wealth resides,
There your heart will be too.

Moving Time

It is the time. Moving time. No more to rewind.

Be aligned, or sit and whine. Do not decline.

Box up the keepsakes and clear out the grime.

With haste! Be on time. Embrace the climb.

It is the time. Moving time. Waste no more time.

All Things (A Prayer of Gratitude)

Thank You for Your love,
And all things.
I come with gratitude,
For Your guidance moves me,
Your compassion soothes me,
For wisdom's unveiling,
Profoundly and sweetly.

I am grateful for love,
And all things.

www.ingramcontent.com/pod-product-compliance
Lightning Source LLC
LaVergne TN
LVHW010849200726
843508LV00012B/2821